garden decoration from junk

garden decoration from junk

LEEANN MACKENZIE

COLLINS & BROWN

First published in Great Britain in 2000 by Collins & Brown Limited

London House, Great Eastern Wharf, Parkgate Rd, London SW11 4NQ.

British Cataloguing-in-Publication Data: a catalogue record for this book
is available from the British Library.

ISBN: 1 85585 761 8 (hardback edition)

A BERRY BOOK

Conceived, edited and designed by Susan Berry for Collins & Brown
Limited.

Editor: Amanda Lebentz

Designer: Debbie Mole

Photography: Gareth Sambidge

Reproduction by Hong Kong Graphic & Printing Ltd

Printed and bound by Sing Cheong Printing Co. Ltd

Contents

STRUCTURAL

CONTAINERS

FURNITURE

SOUND & ILLUSION

Finding junk

Since one person's junk will almost certainly be someone else's treasure, it's difficult to come up with a definitive guide to finding junk. In fact, it's usually impossible to find anything if you have something specific in mind, so it's more a case of liking an object on sight, bringing it home, and then finding a use or a setting for it later.

Where you start hunting will depend largely on how much you want to spend and how much time you have. Prices for the same object vary enormously from, say, a car boot sale to a bric-a-brac or collectables shop, and even from area to area. I rather like leaving the whole process to fate, since you don't want to become a slave to your quest for a particular object, and half the fun lies in the surprise or the fact that your find is a complete one-off. There is nothing more tedious than knowing exactly which shop a particular object comes from, the occupational *ennui* of a stylist.

LOOK OUT

Above: *Look beyond fussy fabrics or gaudy painted finishes – think of how that piece of junk will look once it has been stripped down and restored to its former glory.*

Trust your instinct – if in doubt about buying an item, don't do it. Your gut reaction or instinct is the most important thing to follow. Look at items objectively, seeing beyond any disrepair to their potential usefulness in the garden. Try to be realistic about your level of commitment, too, or you'll end up with a garden full of half-restored pieces that begins to look like a junk yard itself!

TREASURE HUNT

Left: *Sourcing junk is a real voyage of discovery – the thrill is that you can never predict what you're going to find next, or where you might find it. The beauty of junk is that each piece is unique, so finding it is a very personal experience.*

KITSCH CONTAINERS

Right: *This motley assortment of enamelware conjures up visions of vast, steamy kitchens.*

BURNT OUT

Above: *This old car engine coil has a sculptural simplicity and wonderful rusty texture.*

PAST MASTER

Above: *This old deckchair somehow evokes the romance of a bygone era.*

SIMPLY SPECIAL

Below: *Reminiscent of Shaker-style containers, these wooden sieves have a craftsmanlike integrity.*

CHEEKY CHIC

Right: *With its rounded middle and short little legs, this stove has lots of character.*

BOOTED OUT

Below: *These old boots
still preserve their
owner's character.*

STILL BOUNCING

Above: *This jaunty spring looks
like it might bounce off any minute.*

Personality
of junk

WELL READ

Above: *Old hardback
fabric-covered books
have an innate charm.*

SHIP-SHAPE

Below: *This
elegant little
anchor looks
great on
dry land.*

IT IS EASY to imagine that a piece of junk has human
qualities or a personality. Since inanimate objects often
have certain characteristics they can suggest narratives, so
that one special quality can be exploited in a
lighthearted way. It's a bit like falling in love with an
object for no apparent rhyme or reason because it may
remind you of a particular moment or tell a story that is
very personal to you. Because junk has a history or past, it is
interesting to imagine who might have owned or used it
previously. A battered, scratched or damaged appearance also
reveals what the object has been through, rather like wrinkles on
someone's face give us a clue as to their character and lifestyle.
The original use of the object can also inspire you to use it in a
witty and unusual way – planting an old bread bin
with wheat-like grasses, for example, makes a
special feature of these plants as well as referring to
the container's former purpose.

Since the junk items you find will generally have
plenty of personality and interest in
their own right, simple planting
schemes usually work best.

Form & shape

THE FORM AND shape of junk is the quality that will be most important to you, since it is the actual substance of it, and informs us of the actual purpose of the object. Because of its aged nature, junk tends to have a more quirky and unusual shape than its contemporary counterparts – it was often handmade, and so has a far more individualistic feel.

Such painstaking craftsmanship does not exist so commonly these days, with our partiality for mass production. Perhaps that's why hand-blown glass bottles and hand-crafted wooden sieves have such appeal – it's because we know how much work has

FORM & SHAPE

Right: *The spiralling form suggests an inherent energy and force.*

Below: *Bashed old watering cans are easy to come by in myriad shapes and sizes.*

FORM & SHAPE

Above: *The curved, hard, cold metal handles of these buckets seem to sum up their strength and solidity.*

Left: *The ellipses of these stacked up terracotta pots have a sensual shape that works well with cool foliage plantings.*

gone into them. On the other hand, whether mass-produced or not, strictly functional objects have their own stories to tell. The rivets and handles of a bucket, for example, are testimony to its function as a sturdy container. They are not designed to be attractive, yet their form is appealing because it has a functional honesty. These utilitarian shapes look most effective when used in groups, often in repeating patterns, because the numbers add to the impact. More elaborate, quirky objects, by contrast, are more interesting to look at and so make more of a feature when used alone.

When considering form and shape, it's important to think about where you position an item in the garden, because the light will continually alter its form as the sun travels across the sky daily and shadows move and change seasonally.

VARIETY OF
SURFACES

Right *A jumble of old
books and baskets
demonstrating the
varied and attractive
texture of natural wood.*

Far right: *Densely
woven jute rope takes
on different
characteristics en masse
and creates a seemingly
solid, yet fluid surface.*

Right: *Having been
left outside, this pile of
corroding nails has
oxidized, creating white
crystalline deposits on
the surface.*

Colour
& texture

Texture is a more discreet element than colour or shape, although obviously they are interlinked. When an object has an interesting texture, it invites us to reach out and touch it, or to examine the look of it more closely as we watch the way the light plays upon its surface. With worn and battered junk, just as with plants, the form and colour of a particular item sometimes belies what it actually feels like, and it is this visual confusion that also makes us want to touch.

From the pitted, ochre surface of rusted metal to the soft, gnarled fibres of old rope to the smooth, living greenness of algae on wood, each has its appeal and can add to the weathered, crumbling attractiveness of a

dilapidated object. Junk that has passed its practical use is generally consigned to the dumping ground in the garden where it is out of sight and out of mind. So if not beaten up and weathered already, it tends to deteriorate to a state where it quickly merges with the natural elements in the hard landscaping, becoming as one with them.

Both the colour and texture of junk can be complemented or highlighted by your choice of planting. There are myriad plants with lovely textures: lavender and rosemary, for example, also have the advantage of smelling delicious as you walk by and brush against them.

Colour & shape

Above: *Different densities in the grain and knots of the wood causes the algae to grow more densely in the softer, more eroded parts, creating a natural patina to the textural surface.*

Left: *Ferrous metals rust fairly quickly when exposed to the elements, creating distinctive colour and gritty texture.*

Planting
themes

THE BEST WAY to approach your choice of planting in visual terms is to try and isolate the essence of a particular plant, which will, of course, be very subjective. You could almost look at it as though you were extracting the plant's perfume or its concentrated soul or personality – which could be its texture, colour, form or the interplay between several of these. So, for instance, the essence of a daisy is its childlike simplicity, a thistle has a spiky aggression and a lily possesses a sleek, curved sensuality.

With colour, almost more than any other element, economy is the key to success. Fussy mixtures or a riot of clashing colours will just create a visual din; it is far better to adopt a policy of less is more, particularly when planting up junk. On the whole all the

planting in this book is very simple because the junk holds usually holds enough interest in its own right. It is a fine balance, based on an interplay between the shape, form, colour, personality of your object and your own personal taste. In this sense it can be interesting to link the narrative of your junk container with the underlying character of your planting. It could simply be visually sympathetic, whether by colour or texture, or it could have an interplay with the narrative.

Just as with your original selection of junk, you need to follow your instincts and your own personal tastes with the planting, too. If an item of junk has a cheeky personality, combine it with a brightly coloured, rambling plant; if it's utilitarian and functional, cool colours and simple sculptural shapes will be the most effective and visually sympathetic.

SHADES OF GREEN

Opposite clockwise:

Nasturtium leaves, black ornamental grasses rising up from 'Mind-your-own-business' and soft but spiky love-in-a-mist.

SHADES OF GREY

This page clockwise:

an unusual variation of Sedum sieboldii, Senecio and Sedum sieboldii 'Variegatum'.

SIMPLE YELLOWS

This page: *Daisies (right) and sunflowers (below) have an appealing childlike simplicity – there's nothing fussy or exotic about their form or colour. These jolly flowers will cheer up any aspect of the garden.*

SHADES OF MAUVE

Opposite (clockwise from bottom left): *Osteospermum 'Whirligig', viola and petunia all share a similar mauvish hue but have very different personalities because of their form. The viola has soft and delicate layered petals, the petunia has a sculptural trumpet-like form and the 'Whirligig's striking petals resemble the spokes of a wheel.*

BRILLIANT RED

Opposite bottom right: *The hot, zingy colours of nasturtiums are the perfect foil for foliage.*

structural devices

Structure is the backbone of a garden and by using devices such as bed edgings, plant supports and topiary

frames, you can create impact both vertically as well as at ground level. You can also utilize junk finds, such

Lead bed edging

LEAD MAY SEEM a rather odd choice for a garden setting – yet since this naturally occurring mineral comes from the earth, it's really quite a sympathetic material to use in the garden. Traditionally, sheet lead was used primarily as roof flashing but it has been usurped by modern synthetic alternatives that are much lighter and far less expensive, especially on a large scale.

Because lead does not decompose and will withstand the vagaries of the weather, it is particularly suitable for outdoor use. Just think of the Georgian lead cisterns that are still in use as planters today, despite having been exposed to the elements for several hundred years. Lead is a fascinating material to work with, being extraordinarily heavy for its mass and yet very pliable. This makes it ideal for this kind of decorative curved bed edging, which is very useful for creating a barrier between the planting and a gravel path.

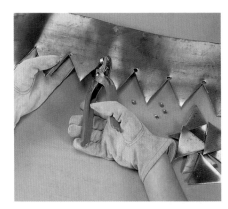

Builder's merchants or roofing suppliers sell rolls of sheet lead in lengths of 3m (10ft) upwards. Even if you plan to edge a large area, I would recommend that you buy several shorter lengths rather than one huge length, as these are much easier to manage. When deciding on the design of your edging, bear in mind that straight edges, such as in this simple coronet design, are the easiest to cut. Creating uniform curves is rather more tricky and rounded edges will require filing.

CREATING THE EDGING

1 Draw your pattern onto a sheet of card and then cut it out to create a template. Wearing gloves, unroll a length of lead, lay the template on top and trace the outline with a bradawl or sharp implement that will score the lead.

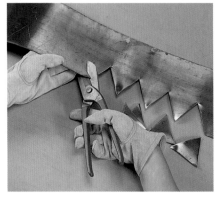

2 Using tin snips, cut along the score lines, taking care not to cut too far. If the lead bends, you can later sandwich it between sheets of paper and tamp it with a wooden mallet or flatten it with a rolling pin.

3 To give the edging an extra decorative element, you can use a rivet or eyelet hole punch to cut out circles in the V-shaped grooves of the pattern. Finally, smooth out any bumps or rough edges with the mallet or rolling pin.

Rope bed edging

ROPE EDGING generally conjures up images of hand-fired Elizabethan rope-effect terracotta tiles – or their concrete modern equivalent. This rope bed edging is a spin-off of that popular design theme as well as being an ingenious and attractive way to protect sprawling plants from constant traffic along the pathway.

Extremely quick and easy to construct, it makes use of natural materials that harmonize with the plants and brick path. I have used cricket stumps as vertical supports because I was lucky enough to find a large number in one go. However, you could use any number of alternatives: I was initially collecting old wooden knitting needles for the purpose. It doesn't really matter what you use provided the materials are in proportion to the size and architecture of your planting and that, more importantly, they fit in with the style. If you have an informal planting scheme, you could choose your supports in a range of different heights and textures to reflect its haphazard nature. On the other hand, if your borders and beds are more formal or if they feature repeated or block plantings, too informal an approach would simply look chaotic.

USING STUMPS

Left: *Robust and ready shaped with pointed ends to be driven into the ground, cricket stumps make great supports for this type of woven edging.*

CHOOSING ROPES

Below: *Jute (top), sisal (middle) and hemp (bottom) are all ideal.*

MAKING THE EDGING

1 *Hammer the poles into the ground to about half their height, spacing them at approximately 25cm (10in) intervals.*

2 *Knot the rope at the base of the first stump and weave it through, back and forth, along the length of the bed.*

ROPED IN

Opposite: *Practical yet rather elegant in its sheer simplicity, this rope edging is deceptively quick and easy to construct.*

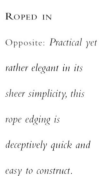

Ivy-covered spring

WITH A LITTLE imagination, you can find a use for the most bizarre objects. These metal spirals are a case in point as they were once part of the mechanics of a car, and were found rusting away in a breaker's yard. Even though at first sight they seemed completely useless and were once intended for a purpose a million miles away from the garden setting, their interesting shape and texture made them a very unusual plant support.

The beauty of these spirals lies not only in their strong simple shapes, but more strikingly in the subtle gradations and textures of the naturally weathered, rusting metal. In fact, car parts are often covered in grease in order to prevent air and moisture from starting the oxidization process. To quick-start the rusting process yourself, you can remove the grease with a proprietary de-greaser and immerse the metal in salt water for a couple of days. Then leave the metal outdoors to rust away at the mercy of the elements. However, there really is no substitute for natural weathering – drips and dribbles that tend to gather on the undersides of wet objects will hold the water for longer, creating those telltale uneven, pitted textures and rich areas of colour that look so stunning next to greenery.

RUSTED SPRING

Above: *The seemingly organic oxidization of this old metal spring is entirely sympathetic to planting.*

TRAILING IVY

Left and right: *The ivy will eventually clamber over the whole spring. The beautiful lime, blue and white markings of this variegated ivy are the perfect foil for the rich varieties in the natural tones and textures of rust.*

Card tricks

F AUX TOPIARY FRAMES are a quick and very easy way to add height and depth to the structure of your planting. Although these are readily available in myriad shapes and sizes, you can really afford to indulge in a little whimsy by creating any shape that takes your fancy or more practically, one that specifically accommodates the particular growing habit of your chosen planting.

A simple diamond shape was my starting point, and I added curly spiral tips so as to avoid any sharp pointed edges. The diamonds reminded me of *Alice in Wonderland,* which in turn suggested a 'pack of cards' theme of diamonds, hearts, clubs and spades, which would be ideal for a small window ledge display. As these shapes are quite graphic, I made the frames two dimensional, but for balls, cones or cubes, you can bind frames together at right angles to give a more architectural feel.

MAKING A FRAME

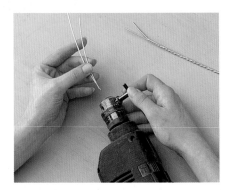

1 *Bend a length of galvanized wire in two and place the ends into an electric drill. Place the looped end around a secure post and gently twist the wire until you have a length of 'twine'.*

2 *With tin snips, cut the looped ends of the wire from the post. Model your wire by hand into the desired shape, then bind the four loose untwisted ends together using florist's wire.*

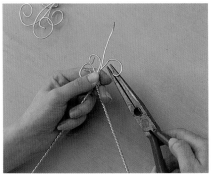

3 *With pointed pliers, trim the wires into even lengths then curl them outwards into spirals so that they are roughly symmetrical to the frame.*

TOPIARY FRAMES

Right: *Jasmine has a wonderfully heady perfume and is ideal for this sort of simple frame because it has a dense spiralling climbing habit with a tight profusion of flowers, so apart from the occasional trim and dead-heading, it can be left to its own devices. The tall florist's buckets have a clean outline and balance the topiary frames perfectly.*

Ladder trellis

OLD LADDERS

Left: *These decorator's ladders had been left rotting in a shed and could not possibly have been used for their original purpose.*

LADDER TRELLIS

Below: *Not robust enough for heavy feet, the rungs of these ladders are perfect for herbaceous climbers. Ivy clambers upwards at a rate of knots, blending in beautifully with the algae and moss that covered the ladders to start with.*

THESE OLD WOODEN decorators' ladders had long outlived their original purpose – and would actually have been hazardous to use. Some of the rungs had collapsed and the wood had become spongy and brittle, like driftwood, where it had been left exposed to the elements for some time.

However, the ladders were ideal as supports for climbing or hanging plants because they were sufficiently strong enough to take the weight and, more importantly, they were so weathered and covered in algae and moss, they would merge unobtrusively into the background.

This kind of support is invaluable to the structure of your garden as it can really provide the backbone to your vertical planting. Ladders can be attached to a wall and used as trellis where evergreen basics such as ivy provide the backdrop or all-year-round interest, while seasonal climbers, such as clematis, jasmine or honeysuckle, can ramble through this to provide lively splashes of colour and scent.

LADDER PERGOLA

Left: *Fixed at right angles, these ladders create an unusual pergola. An old egg basket, planted with trailing skeins of variegated ivy, hangs gracefully from the wooden rungs.*

WIRE BASKET

Above: *Lined with moss, this old egg basket makes an ideal hanging container.*

ALTERNATIVE

Below: *A ladder is used to support the heavy branches of a fruiting fig tree. After a while the ladder even appears to become part of the tree.*

Propped up against one another at right angles, they make a charming rustic pergola, from which you can hang containers of plants from butcher's hooks, or simply allow climbers to ramble through.

To construct the pergola, secure two of the ladders into the ground with a mallet. Slot the top ladder into the rungs of the supporting pair underneath and either bind them together with wire or nail into place. While young climbers are still growing, or if they are seasonal and the wood looks bare, hang baskets of evergreen foliage to maintain interest.

You can even use them to prop and support heavy branches of a tree, such as one that's laden down with fruit. When slender branches droop under the weight, they would usually have to be pruned back, losing you lots of seasonal fruit in the process. But by propping them up and separating the branches, not only do you avoid the need for immediate pruning, you also allow the air to circulate more freely which ripens the fruit faster, thus encouraging more.

Hoe & rake plant support

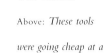

ONE OF MY grandmother's favourite sayings, 'they don't make them like they used to', is certainly true of garden tools. When you consider that old tools were probably in more active service than their modern counterparts, their longevity is impressive. It's surprising how cheaply you can pick up robust, practical tools, often at a fraction of the price of new equipment. I have often been intrigued by some of the different shapes of tools to be found – various tools had very different and specific purposes. A potato spade, for example, was longer, narrower and more curved than a normal spade so as not to damage the crop when harvesting, while a mattock is more efficient at breaking up solid clay soil than any modern tool I have ever tried.

These structures are very useful for providing localized height and displaying seasonal climbers, perhaps in a bed where earlier planting has died back or passed its best. They have advantages over more fixed elements in that they can be easily moved, and would work just as well in a container as in the ground.

If you want to make this a permanent feature it's a good idea to make evergreen climbers the foundation of your display and then add more seasonal colourful climbers. This will ensure a display of attractive foliage all year and hide the bare, dormant wood of seasonal planting. Ivy, evergreen clematis and jasmine are ideal for this purpose but be careful when combining climbers as more vigorous growers will strangle delicate plants.

OLD TIMERS

Above: *These tools were going cheap at a car boot sale.*

Left: *Bound with string, the tools form an interesting pyramid.*

Right: *Forks of a rake – perfect for climbers to ramble through.*

JASMINE TRAIL

Opposite: *Jasmine spirals upwards around the support, creating a stunning and fragrant display.*

FAST CLIMBERS

Below centre: *Boston ivy* (Parthenocissus tricuspidata) *attaches itself to just about any surface by means of sticky tendrils, so it will actually grow up a wall without the need for support. It turns the most wonderful shade of crimson in autumn.*

Far right and below left: *Jasmine is a quick and able climber, using its twining tendrils to scramble in a spiralling fashion up any support, smothering it within a season and perfuming any corner of the garden with its heady aroma.*

Top right: *Clematis hook their stems onto the support with the help of curling tendrils, rather like hands, which need wire or the support of another plant quite literally to grasp onto. Clematis are grown for their seasonal flowers, often through evergreen climbers.*

pots & containers

The most obvious use for junk is as containers. From old buckets to sinks to useless kitchen pots, cottage gardeners have been using these as planters for hundreds of years. With a lot of imagination and a little customizing, even items such as boots, books and humble tin cans may be adapted for planting.

Pavilion bird cage

As ATTRACTIVE AS this cage is, I would not like to think of any bird being confined to it. To my mind, it is put to far better and more novel use as a decorative container for plants.

As a rule, I am not very keen on hanging baskets because they remind me of over-the-top civic displays and their riots of clashing colours, but by choosing a fairly minimal colour scheme and plants that suit the volume and character of the container, you can achieve a really pretty seasonal display.

All you need to bear in mind is that you'll require a little patience and dedication in attaining the end result – the flowers will eventually begin to grow through the bars, but you won't be able to force them.

Start off by planting small plug plants, as these are cheaper and take up little space. Make sure you water and feed them regularly and then simply let the plants ramble through the bars of their own accord. Don't be tempted to overstuff the cage in the first instance: the plants will grow to fit the space.

I've used two different sizes of helichrysum for its soft, suede-like foliage, purple lobelia for its deep blue colour and delicate filigrees of leaves and flowers, plus petunias for their sculptural, trumpet-like blooms.

While the plants in your container are growing, it's a good idea to rotate the bird cage occasionally towards the main light source. This will help to achieve a more even coverage and better balanced display, as the plants will naturally gravitate towards the light. Don't worry about trying to get the growth perfectly even – the plants will ramble where they please in a loose and free manner.

SHADES OF PURPLE

Right: *The striking trumpets of petunias make a real statement alongside the more delicate filigree flowers of lobelia, the whole planting softened by helichrysum. The tip of the pavilion bird cage rises majestically from the midst of all this colour.*

PLANTING THE BIRD CAGE

1 *Stain the wood with an outdoor wood stain in a colour of your choice. Pull some bars out to give you easier access and line the sides with moss. Add a few handfuls of compost to provide a base.*

2 *Feed the helichrysum through the bars, alternating the two sizes. As you are planting vertically you quite literally need to plant sideways until you get to the top layer.*

3 *Follow the foliage with the plug lobelia, gently prizing the bars as you go so as not to damage the plants too much, then finish off with the petunias.*

IN FULL BLOOM

Right: *You can
just see the
elaborate carved
stained wood and
curved metal bars
of this elegant
pavilion bird cage
peeping through
the profusion of
mauve flowers and
soft, grey foliage.*

A touch of playful whimsy has gone into transforming this rather pedestrian and useless-looking old bird cage into a stunning hanging display. Whereas the more decorative pavilion bird cage is interesting to look at in its own right and so calls for a prettier, romantic treatment, this rusty old cage did not have as much personality, so needed something a little extra to create real impact. In this case, the cage is used as the frame for the planting, as well as being the main focus for making the visual pun of a bird in a cage.

The combination of faux topiary ivy, trailing variegated ivy and daisies really works well; the childlike shape of the bird in the cage and the cheerful simplicity of the daisies bringing the whole idea to life.

You can easily make your own topiary frame from twisted galvanized wire (see Card Tricks, pages 26–27) or use a ready made one, as I have done here. Such frames can be found at good garden centres. You can even get away with a very basic outline, provided that you regularly feed the growing ivy back into the main body of the frame and prune back the straggly stems. It will actually bush out very quickly, so that you achieve the density of genuine topiary.

While keeping the main body of the bird well trimmed to maintain its shape, feed the stems of the crest and the tail through the bars of the cage and allow them to grow freely.

RUSTY BIRDCAGE

Above: *The bird had long flown this coop when I found it rusting away in a skip. It appeared totally useless, didn't even look particularly appealing but it cost nothing.*

SITTING PRETTY

Opposite: *This jaunty display makes a pun on the original use of the cage.*

FAUX TOPIARY BIRD FRAME

Below: *This frame was ready-made but you can make your own from wire.*

PLANTING THE FAUX TOPIARY BIRD FRAME

1 *Water your bought potted ivy thoroughly and leave for an hour or so. Knock out the soil and break the up the roots a little to allow for new growth, particularly if the plant is root bound.*

2 *Push your frame into the centre of the pot and, starting with the larger ivy, wind the stems around the main outer frame. Ivy is very robust, so don't worry if you snap off a few stems.*

3 *Use the smaller ivy to fill in the detail, such as the beak and tail. Try to encourage the new growth in the direction you wish it to go by feeding it back into the frame.*

Planted metal buckets

ALL HOLED UP

Left: *Old metal buckets and watering cans with damaged or corroded bases make excellent containers – you can often find them at car boot sales.*

PERFECT PARTNERS

Opposite: *Galvanized buckets and hostas complement one another particularly well, since both have strong and simple architectural forms, are sympathetic in tone and look understated yet striking at the same time.*

LEAFY ATTRACTION

Below: *Hosta leaves have a strikingly sculptural simplicity. Those with variegated leaves provide excellent contrast with their plain-leaved cousins.*

HOSTAS, IN MY OPINION, are the kings of the foliage kingdom, stretching the notion of greenness by displaying it in shades from zingy lime to cool blue, often combined in striking variegations.

Since they have such a strong sculptural form and don't need the drama of sunlight to steal the show, hostas make ideal feature plants for shady areas of the garden that are so often neglected. Galvanized buckets with drainage holes drilled into their bases are perfect containers for hostas for practical as well as decorative purposes.

These plants need fairly moist soil and water tends to evaporate more quickly through terracotta, whereas metal is non-porous and will help to keep the roots cool. A layer of gravel across the top of the soil will also help to retain moisture and to deter slugs, which regard hostas as *haute cuisine*. You can use crushed egg shells or, more attractively, mussel shells to the same end, as these are said to hurt the slugs' 'feet'.

Hostas are herbaceous perennials that originate from Japan, China and Korea, and hence they seem to do well in countries with maritime climates. It never ceases to amaze me how they can die down in the autumn to the point of disappearing, only to re-emerge larger than life in the spring.

MUSSEL SHELLS

Above: *Slugs and snails are the arch enemy of hostas and can shred a whole plant overnight. Crushed mussel shells not only look good as a mulch but are an organic, environmentally friendly way of deterring these pests.*

HOSTAS IN BUCKETS

Left: *Weathered galvanized metal and hostas really seem to suit tone another, since both are cool in tone and temperature and rather understated. As such they create a perfect backdrop for this little anchor pitched into surrounding natural cobbles and gravel, creating a nautical yet green scene.*

IN THE CAN

Below: *A watering can with a hole in its base makes an ideal planter.*

HERB BUCKETS

Left: *Various herbs in old metal cans and buckets look perfectly at home in cottage-style gardens*

THRIVING CHIVES

Opposite & above: *A corroded watering can looks charming when planted with chives that have been left to overgrow and flower.*

Even if they have been munched by slugs they will still re-emerge perfectly formed. You will easily find a hosta to suit almost any size of container, since they vary in size from being just a few centimetres to several metres wide. Generally, the blue-leaved varieties prefer a more shady aspect while some of the yellow and gold leaved varieties thrive in full sun.

The slightly looser, informal planting scheme shown on these pages is more reminiscent of cottage gardens, which would traditionally have used recycled materials or anything to hand for planting, purely for economic reasons.

So worn-out or holey buckets or watering cans would have been entirely appropriate.

Cottage gardeners would have tended to put the practical before the visual, so aromatic and medicinal herbs such as lavender, rosemary and chives would have been mixed in with foliage plants such as helichrysum and *Senecio cineraria*. However, in my planting, I prefer not to go overboard on a crazy riot of different colours. Instead, I wanted to focus the senses on the mixture of textures in the foliage, the cool, calm mauve and grey colour scheme and the wonderful aroma of the herbs.

Paint tins

PAINT TINS

Above: *More than purely functional, paint tins have an appealing form which is set off by sculptural planting.*

THE IDEA OF buying paint tins specifically to either mix paint or transfer it from one container to another seems to me to be a rather ludicrous waste of a decent tin! To my mind, paint tins are put to far better use and certainly give a great deal more pleasure as hanging containers. Obviously they are not designed to be visually interesting but the simple clean lines have a practical, industrial feel.

They look best when planted in the same vein, that is with plants that are simple and sculptural and, perhaps, choosing just one type of plant. I often refer to this as 'bachelor planting' because it's a no-frills, unfussy approach.

Miniature narcissi provide a welcome splash of colour in the early spring and planted up in these paint tins are given a modern, simple edge that is both easy to achieve and virtually maintenance-free.

Seasonal bulbs are traditionally planted in window boxes or beds but if you don't have these and you want to add some vibrant colour at eye level without having to spend time planting up and caring for fussy hanging baskets, paint tins are ideal. Once you have drilled a few holes in the base of each tin to provide drainage, you can plant bulbs in them, or just buy ready grown plants to transfer into them, then simply replace them once they are past their prime with the appropriate seasonal planting of your choice.

Once the miniature narcissi had flowered, my paint tins were consigned to a dumping area in my garden where I entirely forgot about them for a particularly wet few

PLANTED TINS

Right: *This simple but strikingly modern yellow, green and silver display would look particularly good in a modern city roof top garden.*

months. It was a plethora of slugs and snails lurking in this area that finally persuaded me to clear up and throw away all the dead vegetation. This was a rather disgusting chore – but it did bring the paint tins to light again! They had rusted all over and were covered in the most beautiful vibrant oranges, ochres and rich browns, giving them a completely different feel to their previous display and so suggesting a very different planting approach.

There is something prehistoric and otherworldly about these succulents. They have the colouring and texturing of sempervivums yet a structure and form that doesn't really look very 'plant-like' – it's almost as though they belong underwater, or even on another planet!

The soft colouring and fleshy texture of these plants is a good foil for the gritty, pitted oranges of the rusty tins.

SPIKY SUCCULENT

Left and above: *This unusual variation of* Sedum sieboldii *looks tough and and spiky, but is actually very soft and succulent, which invites you to touch it just to find out whether it does feel as it seems. En masse, the stems look just like a nest of writhing caterpillars. In close-up, you can really see how soft and delicate the stems are.*

FLESHY-LEAVED SEDUM

Right: *This* Sedum sieboldii *'Variegatum', a tuberous perennial with rounded, fleshy blue-green leaves splashed with pinky red edges in whorls of three, looks particularly attractive against the rust-coloured tin.*

Catering tins

THIS HAS TO be the simplest container with the simplest planting scheme imaginable, yet beautiful in its utter unpretentiousness. Some people regard mind-your-own-business as weeds as they will grow from only the tiniest fragment and spread rapidly but there is a simplicity in their uniform texture combined with their contrasting coloured foliage that really suits these containers. Sempervivum, more commonly known as house leeks, also look great in tins. Exploit the tonal differences and sculptural forms of these plants by alternate repeat planting to create a modern dynamic display. The tight rosettes of succulent leaves are often flushed with deep mauve-pinks and reds, and so provide subtle colour that contrasts well with the shiny aluminium surface of the tins.

CATERING TINS

Above: *Sempervivums were once planted on roof tiles to ward off lightning and, in more sinister fashion, witchcraft. They are very low maintenance, requiring a minimum of soil in which to root and very little water.*

PLANTED TINS

Left and right: *You could afford to edge a whole border or top a long wall with these semi-rusted, catering-sized tin cans placed in a line with alternate dark green, grey green and lime 'Mind-your-own-business'.*

Enamel containers

FROM THE LATTER half of the 19th century through the first half of the 20th century, enamel pots, pans and paraphernalia reigned supreme in the kitchen. Hardwearing, relatively light and portable and, as a result of mass production, very cheap, enamelware was used in households all around the world. It wasn't until the late 1950s that enamelware began to go out of fashion as people turned to lightweight plastics and stainless steel.

These days the more decorative and ornate items, such as early French storage containers, have become quite expensive and collectable but if you stick to the basic domestic pots, pans and colanders, you can round up a good collection for very little outlay. I really enjoy collecting old kitchen equipment since, for me, it evokes the simplicity and charm of a bygone era. I often find myself buying mysterious-looking items out of sheer curiosity, because I love trying to work out what they were originally used for.

The only drawback of using enamel pots and pans as containers (colanders, of course, are fine) is that they lack drainage. However, this is very easy to rectify by drilling a few holes (see below). The effort is well worthwhile, since enamel is an effective insulator and will help keep soil cool, very much like a ceramic glaze. Another bonus is that you can find enamel containers from tiny egg cups to vast enamel baths, so size is really no object.

OLD ENAMEL

Above: *Look out for enamel kitchenware in second-hand shops.*

POT STAND

Right: *A simple pot stand has its uses outside, as well as inside, the kitchen.*

CREATING THE PLANTERS

1 To prevent the hard, glass-like enamel veneer from cracking, and to give the drill more grip, place a cross of masking tape or sticky plaster over the area you wish to drill. Start a small hole using a bradawl or metal punch and a hammer.

2 Place the metal drill bit on the mark and apply gentle pressure on the slowest speed. Don't apply too much pressure or you will dent the metal. Once the holes have been drilled, remove the adhesive tape or plaster.

3 Cover the bottom of the container with a layer of gravel or broken crocks about 1in (2.5cm) deep. This will allow for drainage and prevent the soil from seeping out during watering. Then plant up in the usual way.

POTTED HERBS AND SALAD LEAVES

Left: Salads and herbs thrive in enamelware on a pot stand, prior to being used in the cooking pot. With a pot stand, you can still enjoy having fresh produce just outside the door, even if you have very little space.

LETTUCE IN A SIEVE

Above: *An enamel sieve makes the perfect container for a lollo lettuce whose frilled burgundy-edged leaves complement the smoothness and colouring of the cream and green enamel.*

JUGS OF HERBS

Right: *Assorted jugs in different shapes and sizes, used to grow a mixture of herbs on a windowsill, are unified by their simple white colour scheme.*

BREAD BIN

Below: *A bread bin planted with wheat-like grasses makes a visual pun on the original use of the container.*

Wooden sieves

THESE WOODEN SIEVES look very much like Shaker-style boxes and indeed they are made in a similar fashion by steaming plywood, although the finishing is somewhat cruder. The sieves make great containers for planting and they need very little doctoring because drainage is not a problem. Since they are available in a variety of sizes, they lend themselves to being used in some form of tiered planter, or are ideal for a hanging herb container if space is limited.

I have adapted two different-sized sieves for my planter. The smaller one has a fine nylon mesh and was probably used to sift flour, while the large sieve has a coarser mesh and so was probably used for soil. In keeping with the simplicity of Shaker style and its preference for natural materials, I suspended the planter with lengths of leather cord knotted at either end (you could also use rope). I then waxed the wood to give it some protection against water and to even out differences in tone in the wood. This makes a perfect space-saving container to hang by the kitchen door so that you have a constant supply of fresh herbs for cooking. Fast-growing herbs like basil, chives, mint and parsley are best and actually benefit from regular picking. Avoid deep-rooted bulbous herbs, such as fennel, as these will not do well in these relatively shallow containers. These planters tend to lose moisture rapidly, so keep plants well-watered.

HANGING HERBS

Above and opposite: *Simple aromatic herbs such as rosemary, chives and thyme, are very much in keeping with the simple Shaker style of this planter and conjure up the fragrances of fresh herb-baked breads.*

MAKING THE HANGING PLANTER

1 *Starting with the top planter, drill two sets of three evenly spaced holes around the circumference of the sieve, at both top and bottom. Then drill just the one set of holes around the top of the bottom planter.*

2 *Cut six even lengths of leather strip or strong twine, tie a knot at the end of each length to prevent the twine slipping through the drill holes. Thread these through from the outside in, then trim off any excess.*

3 *Check that your mesh is not torn and that it will take the weight of soil and plants. If in doubt, repair or strengthen the base by staple gunning a new piece of mesh to the inside. Line the container with moss and compost and plant up.*

OLD SOLDIERS

Left: *The battered and worn appearance of the metal colanders made them far more suited to a practical planting scheme.*

SOFT HUES

Opposite: *Dainty, brightly coloured sweet peas and the soft foliage of helichrysum combine to create a soft and charming display.*

Metal colanders

ALUMINIUM COLANDERS and wire salad shakers make ideal hanging baskets as they can take a fair amount of weight, so won't restrict your planting choice, and they have the advantage of longevity. Because the wire basket was fairly delicate, I reflected this in the planting by using two different sizes of helichrysum for its soft, grey, suede-like foliage, and sweet peas for their soft delicate pink, mauve and plum-coloured flowers. The helichrysum provides the evergreen base for the sweet peas and all I did was to push a few seeds into the existing container to provide the pretty seasonal colours.

The rather worn-looking colanders had a more humorous feel, and made me think of helmets that had seen one battle too many. I thus decided to put them out to grass as herb planters, giving me fresh herbs on tap, together with the most delicious aromas.

SALAD SHAKER

Below: *The delicate look of this wire colander called for subtle planting (opposite).*

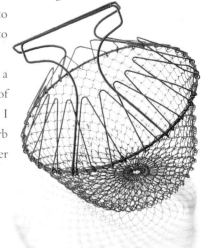

Wire rack

WIRE VEGETABLE RACKS can be used to provide instant splashes of colour vertically without having to attach anything to existing walls; they are free-standing yet very sturdy. You can line and plant them as you would a hanging basket – taking into account that the racks are fairly shallow so cannot take deep-rooted planting. Line the rack with moss first, then cut some dark coloured polythene to size and use that as a second lining. The attractive-looking moss will then be visible through the mesh, while the polythene will prevent water evaporation. Because the wire rack seemed quite Mediterranean in feel, I decided to go for a simple bold splash of red to contrast dramatically with the dark green permanent ivies. Even a dull shady corner on a rainy day could not help but be cheered by such a jolly display.

BUSY LIZZIE

Above: *Busy lizzies are rather common or garden flowers, much used in fussy, over-colourful hanging baskets, window boxes and borders. But if you stick to one rich colour, they can be used very effectively to bring a bold splash of colour to a shady area, or an evergreen feature.*

WIRE RACK

Right: *This old vegetable rack is quite robust and so makes a sturdy planter.*

MEDITERRANEAN COLOUR

Left and opposite: *The combination of the deep greens and rich reds makes a dramatic statement. The hot colours look particularly vibrant against the background of a sunny wall.*

Planted books

IF YOU HAVE ever had books partially destroyed by damp, don't throw them away – put them to another use and create planters from them. You can achieve an effect that is beautiful, sculptural and offers a rather interesting take on the dominance of nature over culture. The longevity of these bookish containers is limited, since they do decompose relatively quickly, but this process is in itself rather fascinating and you could even argue that you are returning the books to whence they came, albeit in the loosest sense of recycling.

Just in case you view it as a sacrilege to waste old books in such a cavalier fashion, you could always use old telephone directories, which most certainly wouldn't have any further function. They may not have quite the intrinsic visual charm of old books, but they do have the bulk to make substantial and solid planters. You can make the books look more warped by weighting them and soaking them in water, or you can wait for nature to produce a more natural warped wave effect. You'll find that the book binding glue will also slowly seep down and help to solidify the container. 'Mind-your-own-business' is perfect for this type of container as it rambles over the jumble of books looking rather like an overgrown ruin.

WAVES OF PAPER

Above: *This warped wave effect occurs as a result of the pages of paper stretching when they are wet and shrinking unevenly when they dry out again.*

OUT OF PRINT

Above: *Old books are beautiful objects in their own right, so if they are damaged or otherwise useless, put them to good use as unusual containers.*

MAKING THE BOOK PLANTER

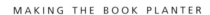

1 *G-clamp the book to a work surface. Using a large wooden drill bit, drill four holes on a slow speed (too fast and you may set it alight).*

2 *With a fine-toothed wood jigsaw blade carefully cut out a rectangle, joining up your holes and moving the G-clamp round as you go.*

GARDEN TOMES

Right & overleaf: *This simple planting scheme of 'Mind-your-own-business' in books works so well because it is quirky, yet understated.*

Puss's boots

THE INSPIRATION FOR planting these old boots with grasses actually came from my cat! I had become increasingly exasperated with him because every time I tried to grow any decorative grasses, he would munch his way through them, making them look dog-eared, ragged and distinctly unattractive.

The only solution seemed to plant something specifically for him to graze on. When I came across an old pair of boots left outside the back door, I hit upon the idea of using them as a container. They certainly couldn't be worn any longer and I thought that they made rather a whimsical and humorous reference to 'Puss in Boots'.

It's possible to buy grasses specifically for cats but rye or wheat grass seems just as palatable, and is readily available from health food shops. All you need to do is soak the seed overnight, plant in a small pot and cover with about 1cm ($^1/_2$ in) of sieved soil, then place in dark warm spot, such as an airing cupboard, to allow the grass to germinate. When it is about 2cm ($^3/_4$ in) high (it will look a pale whitish yellow at this stage), put it in a sunny position where within a couple of hours it will turn a vivid lime green as the chlorophyll is produced.

The grass grows extremely quickly, sprouting up in a matter of a few days or so, so even if it is mowed by an over-enthusiastic, vegetation-loving moggie and starts to look a bit tatty, it is really quick and easy to sprout a fresh crop.

I cannot say that my problem has been completely solved, since my cat clearly has a varied tastes and a rather educated palate. He still enjoys trying different colours, textures and flavours, and has a rather peculiar penchant for purple flowers – but at least now he has one thing on the menu of his very own! You can use ornamental grasses if you don't have a cat and simply like the idea of boots as a quirky container.

Tea & coffee pots

SMALL, UNUSUAL CONTAINERS make a charming display on a narrow windowsill or shelf. Old-fashioned hotel catering ware is easy to get hold of because it was once so widely used, and the fact that it now tends to look rather worn and bashed after years of service gives it even more character. The pots themselves conjure up for me a scene from a Graham Greene novel of great aunts taking tea and cucumber sandwiches on the verandah of an old colonial hotel. You can't help but wonder how many brews they've made and for whom. Your choice of planting for this kind of container is obviously restricted by space, but if you stick to a simple colour scheme with the use of repetition you can't really go wrong. The pots are all the same colour but have slightly different styles, so by mirroring this in your planting scheme, you can achieve a stylish, unified look as opposed to a messy jumble.

Silver-leaved *Senecio cineraria* and miniature purple violas not only fit these pots size-wise, but their soft and delicate nature suits the mood and seems to be enhanced by the way the shiny yet worn surfaces of the pots diffuse and reflect the light.

PLANTED POTS

Left and below: *With their very different styles of spouts and handles, all these pots seem to have personalities of their very own.*

OLD POTS

Above: *Having lost their lids, these tea and coffee pots cost next to nothing, as they obviously would no longer be used to make a decent brew.*

Formal firegrate

I FOUND THIS FIREGRATE rusting away in a field, looking rather pitiful and just too self-important to have been abandoned in such ignoble surroundings. It was crying out for a revamp – even though I had no fireplace at the time. An hour or two's work with wet and dry sand paper revealed elegant solid brass legs and finials and a coat of fire-proof paint gave a sophisticated black, forged-iron finish. Because the grate had a kind of 'stately home' formality, box (*Buxus*) topiary seemed the obvious planting choice, especially since it can give a formal feel on a small scale. The evergreen box and ivy combination is perfect for lazy gardeners as both look good all year round and need only a little clipping to stay in shape. All that's needed to plant this sort of container is a lining of moss followed by a plastic liner with drainage holes which is filled with compost. Top this off with a dressing of cocoa shells. These not only look good and help retain moisture, but will eventually mulch down to feed your plants and have the added bonus of smelling like chocolate when wet.

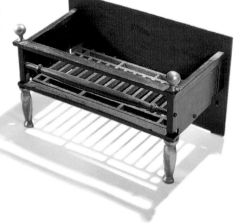

PLANTED FIREGRATE

Left: *The formality of the firegrate gives a sense of grandeur on a small scale, and so suggests planting that will live up to its hauteur. Box topiary is traditionally associated with the formal knot gardens and parterres that feature in the grounds of many stately homes.*

FIRE GRATE

Above: *Usually costly, this firegrate was a real find. Even though in a sense it might have seemed worthless to me, because I didn't have a fire place, it makes a very elegant planter.*

PLANTED DETAIL

Right: *The ivy almost cloaks the structure of the grate but the shiny brass finials rise up through swathes of foliage with a slightly self-important air.*

Nasturtium stove

POT BELLIED
STOVE
Left: *Full of character
and with a really
distinctive and
appealing shape, this
neglected old stove
deserved a lot more
than being left to rot
and rust at the bottom
of garden.*

THE WONDERFUL THING about this little stove-cum-barbecue is the fact that it
is probably already rusting away in your garden, having not been used for years.
There can be few of us who haven't left such things outside when we should have
brought them indoors for the winter, and fewer still who can't
say that they haven't felt guilty for never getting round to
cleaning them up. But I did feel that this stove, with its pot belly
and legs that look as though they might scamper off at any
minute, just had too much personality to ignore. I thought that
nasturtiums, which are also full of character and vividness,
would make the ideal partner for such a stove. The idea of
cheeky planting for a cheeky stove was too much fun to ignore.

PLANTED STOVE
Right: *The strong
citrus yellow, orange
and red colours zing
out in chaotic
profusion against the
green background.*

   Once nasturtiums get going, they ramble off where they
please, so are definitely not plants for those wanting to remain
in control. They are incredibly easy to grow from seed, which is
very useful if you want to jazz up an existing evergreen container. They tend to flower
best on poor soil so don't need feeding and will self-seed in warmer climes, spreading
prolifically if not contained. Aphids are very fond of the succulent stems so either
spray them with a very mild solution of washing up liquid or, if you can bear to wait,
lady birds and ants will soon polish them off.

junk furniture

here are many ways in which junk furniture can be used in the garden, no matter how dilapidated it might

ppear. Less damaged items can be revamped to make comfortable, stylish garden seats, while even those

hat look like completely lost causes can be adapted to provide novel platforms for plants

Reclaimed wooden chairs

OLD WOODEN GARDEN furniture has an innate appeal that modern plastic imitations lack. It tends to have a more complex, quirky structure – often coming with detachable foot rests and even side tables that would have been *de rigeuer* for the early evening gin and tonic on that colonial cruise or verandah.

No matter how old or dilapidated the chair happens to be, it is always worth renovating, especially since it really isn't too much hard work to give it a stylish new look. Usually the first part of a chair to wear out is the upholstery, particularly if it has been left outside. Many will be thrown out at this stage – yet it is a very simple task to recover a motley collection of chairs with stout cotton duck or canvas. It does not matter that you have different styles of chair or different types of wood because if you keep to matching, plain fabrics you will achieve a stylish sense of unity for very little outlay.

The original style of the chair should suggest the way in which it should be upholstered and the appropriate fabric (see overleaf for fabric suggestions). The usual way of fixing fabric to a wooden frame is to use upholsterer's tacks (as shown below).

1940s CHAIR

Above: *The original folding chair, before being recovered.*

MATCHING CANVAS CHAIRS

Opposite: *Cleaning up and waxing the wooden frames and covering the chairs with unbleached calico gives them a stylish new look.*

RENOVATING A CHAIR

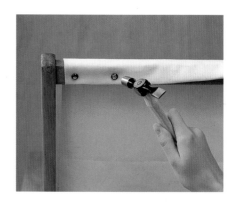

1 *Wrap medium-grade sandpaper around a block of wood for a firm grip and sand off the old varnish. Rub the metal rivets with wet and dry sandpaper to remove as much rust as possible.*

2 *Once the chair has been sanded, apply beeswax liberally with a soft, lint-free cloth. It is best to apply at least three coats, allowing each coat to dry for approximately one hour.*

3 *Measure your fabric and hem the edges if necessary. On the top edge of the chair back, fold the material under and hammer in tacks 5cm (2in) apart. Repeat on the bottom edge.*

The frame of this deck chair had weathered to a wonderful bluish-grey hue, reminiscent of driftwood. This suggested a slightly nautical theme, so the chair has been recovered with a strong cotton fabric in a bleached-out shade of blue, using eyelets and rope.

You don't have to use only traditional methods of upholstering – chandlers are a very good source of inspiration. This covering is reminiscent of sail rigging, which is an ideal reference because it is so tough and has been specially made to withstand the elements. The metal eyelets and rope are strong and sturdy, so that there's no danger of the fabric coming away from the frame and sending the occupant overboard.

The fabric is secured by binding rope around the frame and knotting it at the back.

OLD DECKCHAIR

Above: *Old deckchairs are usually easy to come by because they are often discarded if the fabric is damaged or worn out.*

MAKING THE EYELET HOLES

CHAIR FABRICS

Below: *Any natural material that is strong and has a tight weave is suitable for recovering garden chairs. Below (listed from left to right) are unbleached calico, cotton duck, mattress ticking, chambray and denim.*

1 *Measure your fabric; cut it and hem if necessary. Pierce small holes along the top and bottom edges of the material, about 8cm (3in) apart.*

2 *Use an eyelet punch to seal the eyelets and washers around each hole (follow the manufacturer's instructions). The metal eyelets and washers secure and strengthen the holes.*

RECOVERED DECKCHAIR

Left: *This comfortable old chair is perfect for relaxing in a quiet corner of the garden on a sunny afternoon. The distinctive rope and eyelet fixing is a reminder of sail rigging and was inspired by the original weathered condition of the chair.*

Bamboo deckchair

BAMBOO IS A WONDERFULLY versatile material, having very strong, long fibrous strands with great tensile strength, particularly *en masse*. Sold as humble plant stakes or supports at most garden centres, bamboo is commonly used in the construction of furniture, flooring and decking and is even used as scaffolding in some eastern countries (a real test of its strength). It is not a good idea to use green bamboo as it still contains a lot of moisture, so bends too easily. You could use plain dowelling, although it doesn't boast the colour variations and uneven knots and grain of a natural material.

It is best to leave the wooden frame of the deckchair unstained or use a clear varnish or wax to allow the subtle colour variations of bamboo to shine through. The simple, slightly crude finish of the chair is rather zen in feel – this is definitely a case in which less is more.

EASY LOUNGING

Below and right: The fact that bamboo has so much give yet is incredibly strong makes it ideal for furniture. This chair is extremely comfortable because it offers so much support, yet moves with the body at the same time.

MAKING THE BAMBOO SEAT

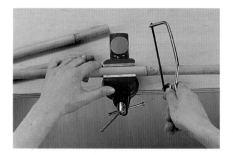

1 *Allowing for a 2.5cm (1in) gap either side of the frame, measure length of slats. Place pole in a vice and cut to size with a junior hack saw.*

2 *Using an electric drill with a wood drill bit on the slowest speed, make a hole either side of the bamboo pole 2.5cm (1in) from each end. Little pressure is needed, as the bamboo is hollow.*

3 *Using strong string, thread poles together, knotting at least twice between each. Drill two holes in the top of the chair frame and two at the base, thread string through and knot securely.*

Wooden church bench

Old JUNK FURNITURE that has outlived its practical use indoors can be adapted with a little imagination to provide unusual features in the garden. Damaged chairs and benches make excellent platforms to provide height, support and structure for plants. You can use them as mini movable theatres for specimen plants or simply as a stage for displaying seasonal colour in its prime. This neglected church bench not only had no seat, but seemed too long and narrow to be of much use without major reconstruction. But it transpired that by creating a plywood base into which pot seats could be sunk, it would be easy to utilize its length to create a potting bench. This is an ingenious way of creating interest at seating level without having to build raised beds and, of course, has the advantage of being easily moved either to hide an ugly area of the garden or liven up an area of evergreen planting with bright splashes of seasonal colour. The pots contained within the frame are also movable, and can be rotated according to your mood. Practically, raising pots off the ground is a good idea in that any bugs have got slightly further to go, you won't break your back grovelling around at ground level and you achieve better air circulation and drainage for your plants.

MAKING THE POTTING BENCH

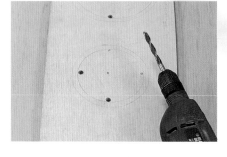

1 Using plywood off-cuts of a width that will fit across your bench, place a selection of pots on top and draw around the circumference of each.

2 Using a wood drill bit, drill four outer holes and then one central hole, making the latter large enough to accommodate a wood jigsaw blade.

3 Rest the plywood between two firm surfaces and jigsaw out your circle, following your pencil line and joining up the holes. Repeat the process for the next pot circle.

4 Once you have cut the holes, use some medium-grade sandpaper to sand down any rough edges and remove splinters. Then simply slip your pots into the holes.

DISUSED BENCH

Above: *This old bench did not look very promising initially, yet with just a little work, it was quickly transformed into a really useful and attractive piece of garden furniture. The off-cuts of plywood used to hold the plant pots are readily available from timber's merchants and cost next to nothing.*

BENCH MARK

Right: *Trailing ivy and small box topiary provide the constant evergreen element while blood red and fuchsia pink geraniums give a vivid splash of dramatic colour.*

RIOT OF COLOUR

Far left: *Bright clashing colours can work well to provide a dramatic theatrical display. However economy is the key to its success. I find that no more than two hot colours with similar tonal values and colour saturation work best.*

DETAIL

Top left: *Darker wood tones such as the stain I have used in this instance tend to work better with richer, more vibrant colour combinations.*

PLANT DETAIL

Bottom left: *The soft, blood red petals of this garden geranium are guaranteed to add drama and excitement to any display.*

CHAIR IN A BED

Left: *Rather than throw out an old chair, you can use it to provide interest and height in a bed or border where the seasonal colour has died back to leave a bare, gaping hole. The planting obscures and softens the actual structure of the chair, looking almost like clothing through which you get occasional glimpses of the body beneath.*

Potted daisy shelf

ACCORDING TO THE market stall holder who was selling this peculiar shelf, it originally came out of an old hospital and had been used as a kitchen draining board. Years of scrubbing with strong bleach had obviously prevented any rot or mould growth and left a lovely, whitish-grey patina, thus suggesting a very clean and simple planting scheme.

As the patina of the raw wood was so beautiful in its own right I did not feel the need to colour or stain it in any way and although this meant that my choice of planting would be fairly restricted to pale delicate colours, the interest would lie in the interplay between the subtle nuances of the planting and the shelf itself rather

DAISY DETAIL

Below: *Cheerful white flowers rise out of delicate silver foliage on long thin stems.*

DAISY SHELF

Right: *Daisies have a very innocent charm and if dead-headed regularly will flower all through summer.*

than the contrast and drama of the church bench and hot coloured geraniums. This piece of furniture was extremely unusual in that the holes were already in place so all that needed to be done was to fix the shelf to a wall and find appropriately sized pots to slot into it.

It makes a very useful little stage for raising plants into the line of vision and to make a special feature of them, as opposed to using more traditional wall pots.

Do remember to place a decent layer of gravel or finely broken crocks in the base of the pots before putting them into this type of raised plant support, as this will prevent a deluge of muddy soil from escaping when you come to water them.

sound & illusion

n the garden we connect with the natural world through all of our senses. Whether we are listening to the

wind rustling in the trees, the trickling of rain, or noticing the way light falls, junk can be used to heighten

our awareness of all the elements that make up our natural environment.

Bath & anchor
water feature

WATER LOVERS

Above and left: *Water lettuces and water hyacinths are extraordinary aquatic plants that have floating roots.*

Tнis sмall water feature is very simple to create and is really just an amalgamation of several different elements that work particularly well together: the tin bath as the stage; the anchor as the actor, and the cobbles, water and planting as the set.

The anchor is the link that makes the whole display effective in that it unites the various elements together in a sort of visual narrative. It is made from the same material as the bath, yet also refers to the cobbles in terms of its original function – man's attempt to wield control over the natural forces of the sea, which in turn formed the smooth cobbles. The cool, weathered, beaten metal of the bath and anchor provide the foil for the warmer colours of the cobbles which vary in tone from deep grey to taupes and creamy whites.

BATH & ANCHOR

Above: *By pulling together different elements, none of which would work alone, you can create a mini set with a watery theme.*

Bucket & cobble fountain

WATER IS ESSENTIAL to our existence, which is perhaps why we are so attracted to it in its most pure and natural form. It somehow heralds the start of spring and regrowth as the snow begins to melt and starts to trickle down mountain streams. Cobble fountains have become increasingly popular in recent years because they are an easy way to incorporate a small, contained and safe water feature in the garden and achieve that wonderful tranquillity of trickling mountain streams. The water pumps themselves are fairly small if you stick to the lower voltage types which means your choice of container is much wider, but this does restrict the flow to something akin to a trickle as opposed to a gush; to my mind an altogether more soothing sound.

The added advantage of the smaller pumps is that they are quieter, so they don't drown out the pleasant sound of trickling water with whirring electrical pump noises. In fact, some of the larger, more elaborate pumps can sound a bit like sinking vacuum cleaners and are far from soothing. I have used my trusty holed metal buckets again, stacked up in a tier with cobbles wedged in between to support the whole ensemble. It doesn't matter how many containers you use as long as they all rather obviously have holes in the base (apart from the one at the very bottom) to allow the flow of water to circulate. If you start with a layer of larger cobbles in the base of each bucket, then place the next smallest sized bucket on top and infill the

OLD BUCKETS

Far left: *Old galvanized buckets come in various shapes and sizes which make them ideal for this sort of tiered water feature. The rivets and handles on these buckets are purely functional, yet the way in which they are constructed and welded has an innate charm.*

WATER FOUNTAIN

Left: *By simply using cobbles in different sizes to infill the sides, you can build up and secure the whole display while still allowing the water to be pumped around effectively.*

sides with smaller cobbles, there will be enough space for the water to pump through, but it is a good idea to scrub the stones first, as grit can clog up the filter, and the style of the water feature needs to be clean and sparkly, not murky. The metal of the buckets and the warm hues of the cobbles are tonally very similar, giving a subtle feel to the feature that makes it particularly suited to a shady or dappled aspect. Pumps are not difficult to install, but they do need a safe electrical supply with exterior duty leads and fittings, so employ a qualified electrician to sort out the cabling for you.

WATERING CAN & STONE FOUNTAIN

Left and above: *The trickling water not only has a soothing sound but highlights the curved shapes of the can and the cobbles, because it catches and reflects the light.*

Glass bottle
water chimes

SETTINGS FOR

WATER CHIMES

Right: *Suspend the*
bottle chimes from a
sturdy branch in an
uncluttered space. The
purple coloured water
will dilute and
eventually overflow as
it rains, giving you a
very personalized
water gauge.

THESE TINKLING WATER chimes are both wonderful to look at and soothing to listen to. You can find a good range of inexpensive old bottles in a variety of interesting shapes and sizes in junk or antique shops. Originally, many of these would have been used for scientific and medicinal purposes, or perhaps as containers for cosmetics and domestic products – here, old medicine bottles have been adapted to make the chimes.

Unlike the cutlery chimes on page 101, the water chimes have a practical use: they collect water and can be used to indicate how much rain has fallen, as the coloured liquid dilutes and the vessels fill up. It doesn't really matter that they are not calibrated, because over time your own personal experience of the weather, the amount of rainfall and how it affects the chimes will give you your own yardstick, or personal rainfall gauge, to the changing seasons.

The actual structure for the mobile is extremely simple to make and is created using exactly the same method as for the old cutlery chimes (with armature wire and metal twine).

CHOOSING GLASS

BOTTLES

Above: *Search out*
an interesting
and unusual
variety of bottle
shapes from which to
make your display,
and partially fill
some with coloured
water for a more
dramatic effect.

MAKING THE WATER CHIMES

The hanging structure for the chimes is created from two 10cm (4in) lengths of armature wire secured with metal twine.

1 *Cut a few lengths of florist's wire, making them between 14-25cm (5-10in) long. Wrap each piece of wire around the neck of a bottle a couple of times.*

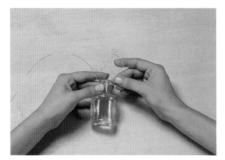

2 *Tie a loose knot and loop one end of the wire to the opposite side of the neck, so that you have two equal lengths of wire from which to suspend the bottle.*

3 *Twist the two wires together to prevent the bottle from spinning and then attach to the armature wire frame. Fill some of the bottles with diluted food colouring, if desired.*

Old cutlery
wind chimes

WIND CHIMES HAVE A wonderful way of linking the changing seasons with our sense of hearing, rather like sound barometers. They are used in many different cultures for a variety of reasons: to scare off birds, as charms, or to ward off evil spirits. It is best to use silver-plated cutlery for these wind chimes because it is deceptively soft and easy to bend; odd forks and spoons are readily available in junk and antique shops and they are surprisingly inexpensive.

Any small household objects of a suitable size and weight can be adapted for the chimes (see Water bottle chimes, page 98), but the most important quality to look out for is the resonance of the object. Silver cutlery chimes with a soothing sound and reflects light very effectively. Simple cutlery looks great when decorated with glass beads, such as the turquoise ones used here. More elaborate cutlery often looks far more effective if left plain.

Rusty old tools, nuts and bolts also make wonderful, rustic chimes that have a pleasant, gentle resonance. Since they tend to be heavy, make sure that you hang them from a fairly robust tree.

SETTINGS FOR CHIMES

Left: *Rusty old nut and bolt chimes blend in soothingly with the natural colours in the garden. They also have a very mellow, pleasant sound.*

Opposite: *When displayed among greenery, silver cutlery makes a striking, contemporary display. The spoons sparkle, acting like small mirrors, to bring vitality to the garden.*

MAKING THE WIND CHIMES

The hanging structure for the chimes is created from two 10cm (4in) lengths of armature wire secured with metal twine.

1 *Rub the narrow part of the handle and bend the cutlery by hand – use pliers for any intricate bending. Suspend each object using metal twine.*

2 *To hang each object, place in the middle of the twine, wrap the twine around a couple of times and twist the ends together. Feed on glass beads, if required.*

Living light for the garden

CANDLES ARE THE MOST MAGICAL way to illuminate your garden and they are particularly appropriate because they are, in effect, living light. They greatly enhance the mood, form, colour and texture of the architecture and the planting. Garden candles have many uses, from providing simple night-time illumination, to having practical benefits, such as acting as insect repellents. The citrus candles (see opposite) have this double purpose: they burn with a lemon-zest fragrance which not only smells good but also deters insects. Made from melted scented wax and old jam jars, they are simple to create and add a bold splash of colour to the garden.

The old fire bucket (below) is a nice visual pun on its original purpose – it has been filled with green sand and crammed with wax tapers.

GLOWING

FIRE BUCKET

Left: *The wax tapers in this fire bucket provide a burst of exotic, flickering flames. The tapers burn down quickly but create a dramatic spectacle in the process.*

CITRUS STORM

LANTERNS

Opposite: *Citrus candles in jam jars can be used as storm lanterns as well as during the day or night as insect deterrents. Light them with a wax taper.*

Road lamp

ORIGINAL ROAD LAMP

Right: *These old lamps are cheap and easy to pick up because they tend to have rusted away quite considerably and the classic yellow and red hazard colours are so crudely painted that they look ugly and worthless. Stall holders attempting to sell these cannot imagine a use for them and practically give them away.*

ONCE USED TO cast light upon roadworks as a warning to drivers at night-time, these old-fashioned road lamps are still used occasionally to illuminate skips. Of course, if you can find even older examples of lamps that pre-date electricity, these are even easier to customize, since they would have contained naked flames and so were designed to protect the burning lights from the elements. Most also have some kind of integral hanging device.

Because these lamps were designed purely for function rather than for decoration, they have an industrial, utilitarian feel. This makes them ideally suited to modern, city roof-top gardens, particularly when their factory look is enhanced with a lick of silver paint to enhance their functional character. This old lamp could also be used as a container.

REFLECTING THE LIGHT

Right: *By adding a mirror to the door of the lamp you add another dimension and a slight sense of mystery. The reflection not only changes with the flickering of the semi-exposed flame but alters as you move around the lantern.*

REVAMPING THE LAMP

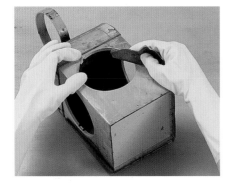

1 *Prize out the plastic windows, then sand off paint and rust spots with fine grade wet and dry paper so the metal feels smooth to the touch.*

2 *Prime with a rust-inhibiting undercoat and finish with matt silver metallic paint. Car spray paint is ideal but any outdoor paint will do.*

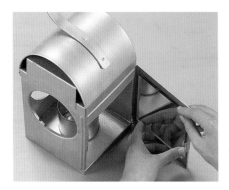

3 *For an extra dimension, add a mirror. Measure the size of the door aperture, cut a piece of mirror to fit and attach to the inside of the door with a suitable adhesive.*

ROAD LAMP

Above: *Hanging from the greenery of a an established fig tree in the early evening light, the lantern really comes into its own. It perfectly reflects the sculptural green forms which seem to change shape as you move around the lantern*

RENOVATED SHIP LAMP

Opposite: *This storm ship lamp would originally have been gas-powered and would have had a curved glass front to protect it from the elements. As it had lost the frontage, I was able combine light (using candles), illusion (with the mirror) and planting.*

Small tin cans were glued to the base inside the lantern and planted with 'Mind-your-own business' to create a very pretty night light.

OLD SHIP LAMP

Below: *Found at a car boot sale, this old lamp had potential.*

Tin can lanterns

WHAT COULD BE more humble and universal than a tin can? They come in all sorts of shapes and sizes, from tiny purée tins through to huge catering containers, and in effect they cost absolutely nothing because we're paying for the contents rather than the cans.

Because tin cans are so utilitarian they seem to look most effective when simply painted in plain, bright colours without any other embellishment. However, because they are so readily available, there's nothing to stop you being more creative and experimental if you wish.

For impact, hang a line of lanterns in alternate colours off crook hooks along the edge of a path. Alternatively, you could place them in a line along an outdoor windowsill, or make a feature of them on a garden bench or table. Not only will they look striking in their repetitive simplicity but they'll also be safer as the flame of the candle is not exposed. It's a good idea to put a few drainage holes in the bottom of the tins to prevent them from becoming waterlogged after a few rain showers.

You can create a decorative pattern by punching small holes into the tin, which allows the light to shine through. Don't make the holes too big, because the naked flame won't have any protection from the elements.

MAKING A LANTERN

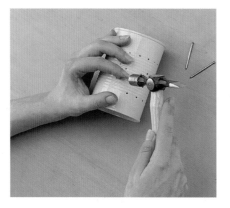

1 *Remove any labels and residual glue, then apply a coat of universal oil-based primer according to the manufacturer's instructions. Next apply a coat of oil-based enamel paint, keeping the coverage as even as possible. Allow to dry.*

2 *Fill the can with water and place it in the freezer until it is solid. This will ensure that you do not dent the soft tin. Next, use a pin hammer and a nail to punch out holes, creating a freehand design around the can.*

3 *To make the handle, punch two holes either side of the can. Using a pair of pliers, cut and bend a length (about 10-15cm/4-6in) of galvanized wire. Thread the wire through the holes and secure.*

Blue glass lantern

BLUE GLASS BOTTLES were once relatively rare and expensive, which is perhaps why today they have been so widely embraced by manufacturers of drinks and cosmetics to package their products. In fact, these days they seem to provide kudos for everything from mineral water to bubble bath.

I have used mineral water bottles here. Their striking colour and unusual shapes make them beautiful objects in their own right, but they can be easily customized to serve a function in the garden. Indoors, all it takes to turn an interesting bottle into a candleholder is to wedge a candle in its neck. Outdoors, you have to approach the bottles from the other end and make use of the fact that bottles without bases make very good storm lanterns. Don't attempt to do this yourself: ask a glazier, who has equipment specifically for such a task that will give a clean, safe cut. Then all you need do is to create an internal coil of wire to support the night lights and suspend the bottles. If you stick to a few simple shapes, the effect is more striking when they are strung up in a line.

DEEP BLUES

Left: *Mineral waters in blue bottles are very popular these days.*

MELLOW EFFECT

Opposite: *Night lights bring the intense blue bottles to life and highlight the wire coil supports inside.*

CREATING THE WIRE COIL

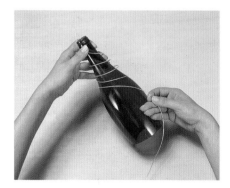

1 *Cut a 1m (3ft) length of galvanized wire and wind this around the outside of the narrower part of the bottle to create a coil.*

2 *Feed the wire into the bottle, ensuring that you leave a straight length at the top from which to suspend it.*

Spring candles

RUSTY COIL

Above: A rusty old spring can easily be transformed into an attractive garden ornament.

THESE RUSTY OLD springs were in a complete tangle in a skip when I found and salvaged them. I had no idea what I was going to do with them initially, they just seemed to have rather quirky shapes and looked like they might spring off at any moment.

There is something inherently cheeky about springs, because even though they are inanimate objects they have such potential force and energy when they are compressed, as in a Jack-in-the-box, for example. Years of service as crucial components of a bed or chair had given all these springs a slightly lop-sided appearance and no matter how I tried to bend them into a more upright stance, they reverted back to their wonky angles.

Their actual structure suggested a form of mini-jardinière, because the coils had a good wide base for support as well as a wide top, providing ample room for some form of appropriate container to be slotted in. After rummaging through all the empty pots and containers in my possession, I finally surfaced with some glass cloches that I had never previously used.

Turned on their ends, they seemed to fit perfectly. I couldn't use them as planters because there was no way of creating any drainage holes, so I decided to put scented wax candles into the cloches to give me a way of displaying these funny little springs.

The cloches don't provide much protection from wind, so the candles need to be positioned in a fairly sheltered aspect to remain alight – but a spitting, flickering flame does rather seem to suit the haphazard appearance of the springs.

NOVEL TWIST

Below: More upright springs make highly unusual stands for plants that won't fight for attention, such as 'Mind-your-own-business'.

COILED CANDLES

Left: *There is an interesting interplay between the colours and textures of the materials used here. The pitted, deep rust of the springs contrasts well with the hard, shiny glass of the cloches and the solid blue wax inside them, creating rather a cool feeling, despite the fact that the candles are burning brightly.*

Mirror, mirror

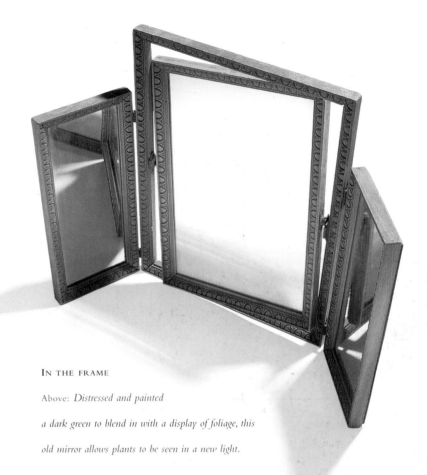

IN THE FRAME

Above: *Distressed and painted*
a dark green to blend in with a display of foliage, this
old mirror allows plants to be seen in a new light.

MIRRORS ARE AN ingenious way to create the illusion of more space in a small garden – especially if used in a discreet and subtle fashion, so it is not immediately clear where reality stops and reflection starts. They are particularly effective at highlighting or leading the eye into a feature plant, so that, in effect, you get double the visual delight for your money. This tends to work most successfully with non-architectural plants because boundaries and perimeters can't be so easily defined – distressing the surface of the mirror also helps to soften any hard reflections. You will find that you soon start looking at things from different angles – perhaps seeing the back or underside of a plant that would usually remain hidden. However, if a plant has passed its prime, simply move your mirror to one that's in better shape.

REFLECTING ON NATURE

Left: *These mauve-blue hydrangeas have a romantic feeling and look beautiful*
reflected in the distressed mirror, whose dark green frame recedes into the ivy behind.

Car wing mirrors

A HIGHLY UNUSUAL AND whimsical display of old chrome car wing mirrors suspended from the branches of a tree actually has a very practical use – they make excellent bird scarers. The traditional method of preventing birds from pecking away at fruit and spoiling a whole season's crop is to use strips of tin foil for their highly reflective qualities, the refractions of the light confusing our feathered friends. Wing mirrors have the same effect, and it doesn't even matter if some have lost their mirrors as the curved shiny chrome reflects the surrounding branches unevenly, distorting their form and creating a kind of moving montage of colour, texture and form. Breaker's yards are the best place to find such wing mirrors but steer clear of classic car parts as these will be expensive.

OUT ON A WING

Above: *This motley collection of wing mirrors originally came from a Morris Minor, a Volvo Amazon and a Triumph Toledo. You can fairly accurately guess at the ages of the cars to which they were once attached by the the distinctive styling of the mirrors.*

LIGHT IN MOTION

Left: *The chrome reflects light and distorts images in such a way that any birds coming close will be frightened off.*

BRANCHING OUT

Opposite: *The reflections, combined with the movement and the shapes of the mirrors, create a sort of moving montage where spacial reality has become quite broken up. In this moving picture, each frame reflects the nuances of the weather, from the sun to rain and cloud.*

Practical issues

ONCE YOU HAVE found your *objet trouvé,* you need to assess what you need to do to it. If you're lucky it may not require too much doctoring – but if it has already been exposed to the elements, by simply leaving it you will allow it decompose or rust even further.

The feel or style of the object should generally dictate how you treat it and there are usually three basic options: you can either try to keep it in its current condition; clean it up and attempt to preserve it; or just let it corrode naturally and make a virtue out of its exposure to the elements. Another option might be to consider ageing it further, but this really only works if you are replacing missing parts of an existing structure with the aim of blending old and new – in which case you want to age the new bits so that they don't look at odds with the original. I can never see the point in ageing a completely new object and then sealing it to preserve its *faux* antiquity. Apart from looking trite it can never really duplicate the real ageing process or the effect of the natural vagaries of the elements themselves, particularly in a garden setting; it would be like trying to paint *faux* lichen on brick or verdigris on copper.

To some extent you can fudge and bodge your way around things, but just be realistic about your limits. For example, if something needs welding, which might be beyond your level of skill or equipment, simply bind it together with string or wire and make a feature of the fact that it looks disjointed and junky. Adapt what you have to suit your purpose: if you have to buy expensive waxes or paints, it defeats the object of spending very little on an item. Manufacturers are very good at bringing products onto the market that are supposedly designed for very specific purposes – but all that differentiates them from any other all-purpose products is the marketing and packaging.

I am notorious for not reading manufacturer's instructions before I start using a product, and indeed you can get some interesting effects by breaking the rules. However, more often than not it all goes horribly wrong, so unless you feel extremely reckless and don't mind whether you damage your object or are fairly sure of the effect you will get, do as it says on the packaging.

All you need is a fairly basic tool kit, much of which can be picked up cheaply from markets or second-hand shops. There is no doubt that mechanization speeds things up but be wary – unless you want to achieve the circular patterns created by the rotation of delta sanders, for example, you will have to finish off by hand.

TREATMENTS FOR WOOD

When you want to combine old and new wood and achieve some degree of harmony, you have two options. First, you can cover the whole ensemble with a paint that will entirely disguise the texture and grain of the wood, or, second, you can treat each type of wood so that they eventually appear to have been part of the same structure. If you take the latter route, you can sand the old wood down until you reach wood

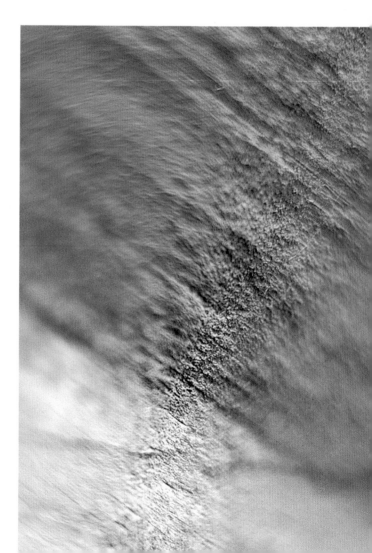

available colours). You could also stain the bare wood in a water-based solution whilst it is absorbent, and then wax over the top to seal and protect. On the whole, I'm not a great fan of varnishes because they just sit on the surface of the wood, rather than feeding or nourishing it, as oils and waxes do. They are not suitable for outdoor use either as they tend to blister and flake quickly when exposed to the elements, which makes them fairly high maintenance. In fact, unless you want a particularly glossy finish, they are best avoided.

HOW WOOD DISINTEGRATES

Wood that has been exposed to moisture will eventually get wet rot. Fungal spores, which are always present, multiply so rapidly that the timber eventually becomes so brittle and spongy that it quite literally falls apart, particularly if it gets the chance to dry out completely. Splitting and warping occurs along the grain where the harder areas of wood dry out and contract at a slower rate than the softer areas.

TREATING METAL

Rust is a form of corrosion that affects ferrous metals, notably iron and steel. It is due to a combination of the effects of water, oxygen and carbon dioxide, hence the reason you get so many variations in the speed and extent of corrosion from area to area. Being a big fan of rust, I very rarely want to treat metal at all. However, some objects do suggest a cleaner, more polished finish and if the metal is thin it will corrode quickly and eventually disintegrate. You can't just paint over rust – you first need to treat it. Sand down any flaking paint or highly pitted areas of rust with a wire brush first. If the rust is bad, finish off with wet and dry paper until the surface is smooth to the touch. If you leave any rust, it will simply bleed through your layer of paint. Then treat the rust with a proprietary rust inhibitor (phosphoric acid) or an aluminium spirit-based sealant (zinc phosphate) which halts the oxidization process. Car spray paint is perfect for a really smooth finish, or you can use enamel paints with a very soft bristled brush so as not to leave any brush marks.

that has not been weathered too extensively to see if you can make an approximate tonal match with the replacement wood. This is only feasible if you need to go down merely a millimetre or two. Alternatively you can treat your new wood to a *faux* weathering process by staining it to an appropriate tone, then applying a coat of *grisaille*-coloured wash (a dusty, bluish-grey hue will usually make a fairly good match). It is best to do this by eye and test a small section, if possible, as wood stains are well-known for looking a very different colour, let alone tone, when dry. Err on the side of caution until you become familiar with the particular qualities of a colour, stain or wax and you can then gradually build up the intensity of the tone because they are transparent, like glazes.

In theory it's important to not mix your materials in the wrong order. For example, an oil-based wax or glaze is fine over water-based but not vice versa. A cheap option to colour or tone wood is to simply use a neutral beeswax or linseed oil as a base and tint it accordingly with shoe polish (for waxes), pigments or even fabric dye dissolved in some tepid turpentine (particularly as there are such a range of readily

drill

delta sander

jigsaw

flat bedded sander

Tool kit

IF YOU intend to renovate the odd item of junk as and when you find something that catches your eye, you will almost certainly be able to hire or borrow the electric, labour-saving tools listed on this page. They are really only worth investing in if you are going to use them on a regular basis. The basic tools (right) however, are handy to have in any tool box – and will certainly come in useful if you want to recreate any of the ideas featured in this book.

ELECTRIC DRILL

This is only essential if you need to drill through metal. It is vital that you use proper drill bits specifically designed for metal – if you don't, not only will you damage expensive equipment but the job will take twice as long. If you are tackling metal, wear safety goggles to protect yourself from sparks.

ELECTRIC DELTA SANDER

This sander serves the same purpose as a flat bedded sander (below) but, with its triangular head, has the advantage of being able to get into awkward nooks and crannies. It's useful for removing flaking paint quickly from inaccessible corners, but it's generally a good idea to finish off by hand as the mechanical action of the sander rotates and thus leaves circular indentations in wood.

ELECTRIC JIGSAW AND WOOD SAW

An electric jigsaw is not essential, but it does take a lot of the strain of sawing by hand. The main advantage of these tools is that they can cut out quite complex shapes from, say MDF or plywood, accurately and quickly.

ELECTRIC FLAT BED SANDER

This extremely useful tool is basically a mechanized version of a cork or rubber sanding block and it is invaluable if you have larger, flattish areas of wood to smooth down. Choose an appropriate grade of sandpaper according to the extent of the wear and tear and the level of finish you require.

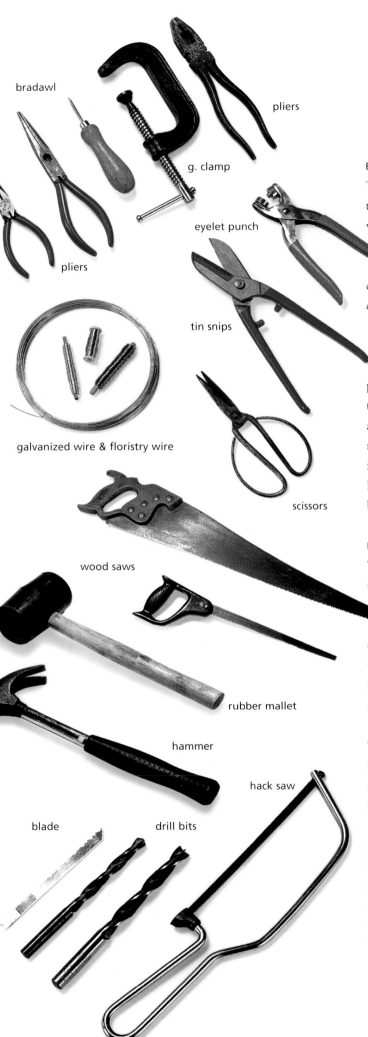

bradawl

pliers

g. clamp

eyelet punch

pliers

tin snips

galvanized wire & floristry wire

scissors

wood saws

rubber mallet

hammer

hack saw

blade   drill bits

BRADAWL

This is one of the most useful tools in my tool box. It's meant to be used to start a pilot hole in wood prior to fixing screws without having to drill a hole first, but it has myriad other uses, from scraping paint out of detailed mouldings to prizing joinery apart. With metal containers that need drainage holes it is useful for marking an indentation before drilling which helps to stop the drill slipping.

G-CLAMP

This is invaluable in securing objects to a surface, particularly if you don't have a proper workbench and intend to use electric tools. Make sure the surface you use is stable and not particularly precious – the number of times I have mistakenly drilled or sawed through my kitchen table has left it looking ravaged! These clamps are also very useful for holding items together while glue dries: no household should be without at least one.

PLIERS

These come in all sorts of shapes and sizes, depending on their intended task. They are used in the delicate process of watchmaking and jewellery tools as well as for industrial jobs that require a lot more brute force. In essence they are a mighty version of a strong pair of hands, with a pincer action to hold things securely. They are essential to prevent you from shredding your own hands on sharp metal or wire.

TIN SNIPS

Designed primarily to cut sheet metal, tin snips are like heavy duty scissors. Ideally you should use pliers to cut wire but if it is particularly tough, tin snips will do the job.

MISCELLANEOUS TOOLS

Strong scissors, different types of wire, wood saws and a hack saw, a hammer and a rubber mallet are all essential items for the junk renovator. It is also vital to ensure that you are using the correct blades or drill bits for the material you are to work on, otherwise you will damage expensive equipment.

Planting suggestions

The plants listed here all do well in containers. They have been chose for one of more of the following: their handsome leaves, interesting form or for particularly attractive flowers. Just a few have been chosen for their culinary delights! Most of them look best planted on their own, for maximum impact.

FOR FLOWER COLOUR

Argyranthemum foeniculum
H 90cm (3ft)
This compact shrub bears pure white daisy-like flowers all summer long. It needs good sun and well-drained soil. Grow from cuttings in summer. You can train this plant to grow into a standard (with a clear stem and a bushy head of flowers).

Dahlia 'Bishop of Llandaff'
H 1m (3ft)
With its dark blackish-red foliage and singularly bright red flowers, this dahlia makes a strong statement. Grow it in full sun and provide it with a few twiggy supports, as the stems tend to droop. After flowering, store the tubers indoors, upside down, in an airy place until next spring when they can be planted outside again.

Lavandula stoechas
H 1m (3ft)
Known as French lavender, *L. stoechas* has particularly attractive purplish spiky heads of scented flowers from early to late summer, and the usual grey green narrow leaves of lavender. Does well in poor soil in full sun.

Narcissus 'Peeping Tom'
H 30cm (12in)
A popular bulb, this produces particularly attractive small, dainty, yellow flowers in spring. It grows well in ordinary soil, which should ideally be kept moist during the growing season.

Nigella damascena
H 45cm (18in)
Known as love-in-a-mist, this cottage garden flower self-seeds very freely. It is grown as an annual, producing its pretty, starry blue flowers in midsummer. There are many cultivars, some dwarf, some with pink or white flowers. Grow from seed, sown in spring.

Osteospermum 'Whirligig'
H 60cm (24in)
This daisy-like, shrubby plant produces its curiously spoked white flowers from spring through to autumn. The flowers have a dark blue centre. Sow from seed in spring or propagate from cuttings in late summer. It needs full sun.

Petunia
H 30cm (12in)
These vigorous, branching half-hardy perennials (grown as annuals) produce large quantities of large, five-petalled flowers in colours from white, pink, magenta, blue and purple. The Surfinia Series of Grandiflora petunias have slightly smaller flowers, but plenty of them, in every shade. 'Surfinia Purple' has magenta flowers with purple veins. Grow from seed sown in warmth in mid-spring.

Tropaeolum majus
H up to 2m (6ft)
This trailing annual is grown for its singularly handsome, waterlily-shaped, bright green leaves and its large bright orange, yellow or red flowers, from late summer to early autumn. It will trail or climb if given a helping hand. Grows best in poor soil in full sun. Sow seed in mid spring.

FOR LEAF SHAPE/COLOUR

Artemisia 'Powis Castle'
H 60cm (24in)
This woody perennial is grown for its delicate silver grey feathery foliage. It needs well-drained soil and full sun, but is susceptible to frost. Grow from cuttings in early summer.

Helichrysum petiolare
H up to 1.5m (5ft)
This trailing evergreen has wonderfully felted, silvery grey-green rounded leaves that trail attractively. Various cultivars offer lime green, variegated or smaller leaves. Does best in sun. Grow from cuttings in summer.

Ophiopogon planiscapus 'Nigrescens'
H 15cm (6in)
Grass-like in appearance, this striking plant, with an impossible name, has almost black strap-shaped leaves. Grow in sun or partial shade. It looks good planted with the dark leaved pansy, *Viola labradorica*.

Salvia officinalis 'Purpurascens'
H 1m (3ft)
Purple-tinged leaves mark this variety out from the common sage, but otherwise it has the same attributes, with aromatic, felted foliage. An excellent culinary herb, it does best in poor soil in full sun. Grow from cuttings taken in summer.

Sedum sieboldiana 'Mediovariegatum'
H 10cm (4in)
This spreading, tender, tuberous perennial is grown for its rounded, waxy leaves that have cream marbling, sometimes with red margins. Small pink flowers are borne in late summer. Grow from cuttings in summer. Needs well-drained soil in full sun, and copes well with drought.

Sempervivum tectorum
H 15cm (6in)
Known as the common houseleek, this tough mat-forming succulent produces rosettes of blue green leaves, with a bristly tip, and red purple flowers in summer. Grow in poor, gritty soil in sun. Offsets will be produced, which can be planted up as new plantlets.

Senecio cineraria
H 60cm (2ft)
Grown for its silvery-grey, felted leaves, this sub-shrub, known commonly as cineraria makes an attractive foil for blue and purple flowered plants, such as pansies and petunias. It does best in well-drained soil in full sun. There are a number of cultivars, including 'Silver Dust' which is smaller with lacy leaves and 'White Diamond' with oak-shaped leaves.

Soleirolia soleirolii
H 5cm (2in)
Known as 'Baby's tears' or 'Mind-your-own-business', this little mat-forming perennial has small pale green leaves. It spreads quickly to make a carpet underfoot in most soils and conditions. There are gold-leaved and silver-variegated forms. Propagate by division in late spring.

FOR STRONG FORM

Buxus sempervirens
H 5m (15ft)
Box, as it is commonly known, is widely used for topiary, as it is slow growing with small, neat evergreen leaves. *B. s.* 'Suffruticosa' is compact and very slow growing. There are many species and cultivars, with differing habits and foliage. *B. microphylla* has smaller leaves and grows only to 75cm (30in). Prefers light shade and well-drained soil. It is fairly drought tolerant. Propagates easily from cuttings in summer.

Cordyline australis
H 3m (10ft) or more
Known as the cabbage palm, this evergreen tree-like shrub has a rounded head of sword shaped leaves on an increasingly long trunk. There are many different forms with striped or coloured leaves, including "Purpurea' with purple leaves. Grow in well drained soil in sun or partial shade. It is not frost hardy and may need protection in winter in colder areas.

Hosta sieboldiana 'Elegans'
H 1m (3ft)
This particularly handsome hosta has waxy, deeply veined, blue-grey leaves, roughly 30cm (12in) long. It makes a really handsome clump of foliage in a pot. In summer, a spire of

lilac flowers rises from the centre of the clump. There are many other hostas to choose from with smaller leaves, some of them splashed with white or yellow. Does best in moist soil in partial shade.

Skimmia japonica
H 1.2m (4ft)
This evergreen shrub has neat glossy dark green leaves and desne clusters of small white flowers from mid- to late spring, followed by bright red cones of berries.

FOR CLIMBING ABILITIES

Hedera helix 'Pedata'
H 4m (12ft)
Known as the bird's foot ivy, this one clothes walls well, with its elegant, long-fingered, grey-green leaves. *H.h.* 'Professor Friedrich Tobler' (45cm/118in) is good for trailing, with small mid-green leaves that have a heart-shaped base. The variegated 'Tricolor' is also popular for hanging baskets. All ivies will cope with very poor soil and deep shade. To propagate, simply take a cutting that has roots attached and plant up.

Clematis
H 4m (12ft) or more
There are many different species and hybrids to choose from, from the small-flowered viticella species to the large dinner plate hybrids like 'Jackmanii'. On the whole, the species clematis are tougher. They need to have their roots shaded and their heads in the sun. *C. montana* copes well with north-facing walls and there are cultivars with white or pink flowers.

Jasminum officinale
H 12m (40ft)
This white-flowered jasmine is not fully hardy, but has wonderfully scented flowers from summer to early autumn. *J.o.* 'Affine' has larger, pink-tinged flowers. Grow in fertile soil in sun or partial shade. Propagate from cuttings in summer.

Lonicera periclymenum 'Serotina'
H 7m (22ft)
Known as the late Dutch honeysuckle, it produces cream flowers streaked with pinky purple that are highly fragrant from midsummer to early autumn. Most do best in partial shade. Prune after flowering to keep it under control.

Parthenocissus henryana
H 10m (33ft)
Known as Chinese Virginia creeper, this one has the bonus of foliage that turns a brilliant scarlet in autumn. It produces best colour in part shade, but will grow in sun or shade in fertile soil. Prune it in summer and again in early winter.

FOR THE TABLE

Allium schoenoprasum
H 30cm (12in)
Known as chives, this member of the onion family is a perennial grown primarily for its succulent little stems, but it bears the usual pretty pale purple rounded heads of onion flowers in summer. Grow in fertile, well-drained soil in sun. Propagate from seed sown in spring.

Ocimum basilicum
H 30cm (12in)
Basil is one of the most aromatic herbs, a tender annual, with pretty, soft rounded green leaves. A purple-leaved form, 'Dark Opal', is particularly attractive. Grow it from seed after frosts have finished. This plant needs a position in full sun to do well.

Petroselinum crispum
H 30cm (12in)
Parsley is not only good to eat, it makes a good decorative edging for window boxes and borders. The tightly curled leaves can be chopped to add to stews, salads and stuffings, and have medicinal properties. Grow in fertile soil in sun from seed sown in late spring.

Index

ACKNOWLEDGEMENTS

THE AUTHOR would like to thank the following people, without whom this book probably would never have got off the ground! Thank you firstly to my twins, *Ellis and Spencer*, for hanging on in there for dear life and for being with me all the way. To my outlaws, *Spy, Graham* and *Jools* for their lawfulness.

Thanks to *Debbie Mole* for her sensitive and courageous design, to *Mandy Lebentz* for untangling my ramblings, and to *Gareth Sambidge* for his stunning photography and boundless sense of humour in the face of adversity. Thanks also to *Susan Berry,* who kick-started the whole book and kept it together when I strayed and to all those friends who let me invade their gardens: *Johnny* and *Tania, Sarah* and *Jactar, Ruthless, Kate* and *Paul* and *Simon* and *Thea.* Thanks also to David Fordham for work on the initial design, to Ginny Surtees for her initial editorial work and to Loryn Birkholtz for her editorial assistance.

Lastly and most importantly, thank you to my husband *Jeremy* for sawing, sanding, drilling, lugging and being general dogsbody for me when the bump got too big; for vaguely tolerating a home that at times looked like a junkyard and for all his love and support.

PHOTOGRAPHY CREDITS

Thanks to the following for their photographs:
Michelle Garrett: pages 21, 37, 38,39, 41, 46-7, 55, 58 (top left hand), 59, 72-3, 80, 88, 92-3, 102 (bottom left), 105, 115.

Polly Wreford: pages 44 (main pic and top right), 56-7, 97, 103.

Lucy Pope: pages 79, 101, 104, 105,